D0459551

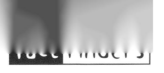

Biographies

Ellen Ochoa
Pioneering Astronaut

by Lissa Johnston

Consultant:
James Gerard
Aerospace Education Specialist
Kennedy Space Center

Capstone
press

Mankato, Minnesota

Fact Finders is published by Capstone Press,
151 Good Counsel Drive, P.O. Box 669, Mankato, Minnesota 56002.
www.capstonepress.com

Library of Congress Cataloging-in-Publication Data
Johnston, Lissa Jones.
   Ellen Ochoa : pioneering astronaut / by Lissa Johnston.
   p. cm. — (Fact finders. Biographies. Great Hispanics)
   Includes bibliographical references and index.
   ISBN-13: 978-0-7368-5438-2 (hardcover)
   ISBN-10: 0-7368-5438-X (hardcover)
   1. Ochoa, Ellen—Juvenile literature. 2. Women astronauts—United States—Biography—
Juvenile literature. 3. Astronauts—United States—Biography—Juvenile literature. 4.
Hispanic American women—Biography—Juvenile literature. I. Title. II. Series.
TL789.85.O25J64 2006
629.45′0092—dc22   2005022580

Summary: An introduction to the life of Ellen Ochoa, the first female Hispanic astronaut.

Editorial Credits
Megan Schoeneberger, editor; Juliette Peters, set designer; Linda Clavel and Scott Thoms,
   book designers; Wanda Winch, photo researcher/photo editor

Photo Credits
NASA/Johnson Space Center, cover, 1, 13, 14, 18, 19, 20–21, 22, 24–25, 27; Kennedy Space
   Center, 5; Marshall Space Flight Center, 23
Photo courtesy of Dr. Ellen Ochoa, 7, 8, 11
Photo courtesy of Ellen Ochoa Middle School, Pasco, Washington/Public Affairs Office, 26
Photo courtesy of Sandia National Laboratories, 16–17

1 2 3 4 5 6 11 10 09 08 07 06

Table of Contents

Blast Off!

The shuttle *Discovery*'s front window pointed straight up into the night sky. Ellen Ochoa held out a mirror to see the launch pad below. In the mirror's reflection, the glow from the shuttle's exhaust was bright as daylight.

But Ochoa had little time for sightseeing. She lay strapped into her seat, flat on her back. She watched the computer. Her job was to help make sure everything was ready for launch.

Suddenly, the engines roared to life. The shuttle's support structure creaked and groaned. The shuttle vibrated. Then, the rocket boosters fired and lifted *Discovery* into the sky.

Ellen Ochoa blasted off in the *Discovery* space shuttle in the dark of night on April 17, 1993.

Ochoa and the crew were soon far above earth. The shuttle's external fuel tank and rocket boosters fell away. The ride smoothed out. Ellen Ochoa officially became the first Hispanic female astronaut in space.

Childhood

Ellen Ochoa was born May 10, 1958, in Los Angeles, California. She was the third of five children. Her father, Joseph, was born in the United States, but his parents were born in Mexico.

Strong Influence

Ochoa's mother, Rosanne, believed strongly in a good education. When Ochoa was a baby, her mother started college. She took one class at a time. Twenty-two years later, she graduated.

Ellen Ochoa was a curious child and enjoyed learning.

School

Ochoa followed her mother's example. She was a good student. She especially enjoyed math and science. When she was in fifth grade, Ochoa thought she might like to be president. She considered becoming a lawyer too.

QUOTE

"My mother influenced me the most . . . Her primary focus was the enjoyment of learning. That's what I got from her example."

—Ellen Ochoa

◄ As a teenager, Ochoa enjoyed taking math and science classes.

Ochoa also enjoyed music. All of the Ochoa children played instruments or sang in choirs. Ochoa took piano lessons when she was 8. She began playing the flute when she was 10. She was in the marching band and concert band throughout high school.

When Ochoa was 11 years old, the *Apollo 11* spacecraft landed on the moon. People all over the world became interested in outer space. Ochoa did too, but she didn't think of becoming an astronaut. At that time, astronauts were men, not women.

FACT!

Ochoa loved to read. One of Ochoa's favorite books when she was young was *A Wrinkle in Time* by Madeleine L'Engle. It is about a girl who travels through space.

Higher Education

When Ochoa was in junior high school, her parents divorced. Ochoa's mother moved the children to La Mesa, California, near San Diego.

In 1975, Ochoa graduated at the top of her class at Grossmont High School. After high school, Ochoa attended San Diego State University.

College offered many interesting classes and excellent teachers. Ochoa had a hard time deciding what to study. She thought she might become a musician or a businessperson. She changed her mind four times.

Ochoa's family gathered to celebrate her graduation from San Diego State University.

Then Ochoa took a **physics** class. She liked the way physics combined math and science. She switched her major a fifth time. In 1980, she graduated with a degree in physics. Once again, she was at the top of her class.

After graduating, Ochoa could have begun a career. But she decided to continue her education. She entered graduate school at Stanford University instead.

QUOTE

"I tell students that the opportunities I had were a result of having a good educational background. Education is what allows you to stand out."
—Ellen Ochoa

Reaching for the Stars

While Ochoa was at Stanford, Sally Ride became the first American female astronaut in space. Ochoa was encouraged by Ride's success. In 1985, she applied to the National Aeronautics and Space Administration, or NASA.

In June 1983, Sally Ride became the first American woman in space. ➤

In the 1980s, almost all astronauts were men.

Ochoa wasn't sure she was right for the job. Most astronauts were men. Most had been pilots in the military. Many were strong and athletic. Ochoa wasn't any of these things.

Thousands of people had applied to become astronauts. Only a few were chosen. NASA did not choose Ochoa. She was disappointed, but she didn't give up.

QUOTE

"[Becoming an astronaut] just seemed like such a great way to combine my interest in research and engineering as well as space exploration."
—Ellen Ochoa

Career Choices

Ochoa earned a degree in electrical engineering from Stanford. One of her professors was an expert in the field of **optics**, the study of light and light waves. Ochoa made optics her specialty.

Ochoa went to work at Sandia National Labs in California. She invented some important ways to use optics. Three of her inventions received **patents**.

Ochoa's next job was at NASA's Ames Research Center in California. She was in charge of writing software for aircraft. In her spare time, she got her pilot's license. In 1987, Ochoa applied to NASA again.

Ochoa and her coworkers at Sandia National Labs did experiments to study light and light waves.

Astronaut Ochoa

In 1990, Ochoa finally was accepted into astronaut training. She began the demanding one-year program at Johnson Space Center in Houston, Texas.

Ochoa had studied hard all her life. In order to be an astronaut, she had to learn even more.

Ochoa learned how to use a parachute in case of an emergency. ➤

"Weightlessness is the fun part of the mission."
—Ellen Ochoa

As an astronaut, Ochoa studied many subjects. She studied geography, the stars, the weather, and medicine. She learned about the space shuttle. Ochoa learned survival skills and about weightlessness. She finished her astronaut training in July 1991.

As part of her training, Ochoa became familiar with the controls in the cockpit of an air force plane. ➤

U.S. AIR FORCE T-38A
A.F. SERIAL NO. 66-
SERVICE THIS AIRCRAFT WITH
JP-4 FUEL IF NOT AVAILABLE, T.
42B1-1-14 WILL BE CONSULTED
EMERGENCY ACTION.
SUITABLE FOR USE OF AROMA

Working in Space

Ochoa's first space flight was in April 1993. She was one of five astronauts aboard the space shuttle *Discovery*. Ochoa was a **mission specialist**. Ochoa and her crewmates studied the sun's effect on the earth's atmosphere. One of Ochoa's main jobs was to operate the shuttle's robotic arm, known as the Remote Manipulator System (RMS).

Space Robot

The RMS is 50 feet (15 meters) long with joints similar to those of a human arm. Ochoa operated the RMS with remote controls inside the shuttle. The controls are like those of a video game.

Ochoa takes a break on the shuttle *Atlantis* during her second space flight.

Ochoa used the RMS to release a **satellite** into space to find data. At the end of the mission, Ochoa used the RMS to recapture the satellite. She performed similar duties on her second space flight in 1994.

> "I never got tired of watching the earth, day or night, as we passed over it. Even though we brought back some pretty incredible pictures, they don't quite compare with being there."
>
> —Ellen Ochoa

Ochoa brought along her flute and played it during her first space flight. ⬇

The Space Station

Ochoa's third flight was in 1999. It was the first time the space shuttle docked with the **International Space Station** (ISS). Ochoa worked on the ISS project for two years before the flight. Her crew trained together for nine months.

Ochoa helped deliver more than 2 tons (1.8 metric tons) of equipment and supplies to the space station. Once again she operated the RMS. During a space walk, another astronaut stood on the RMS. Ochoa worked the controls. Together, they moved large items from the shuttle to the space station.

▲ Ochoa could
see earth from
inside the
International
Space Station.

Ochoa's 2002 mission lasted 11 days. The space shuttle *Atlantis* carried two pieces of equipment to the ISS. The crew of the *Atlantis* docked with the ISS. They worked from inside the space station during the mission. Ochoa and a fellow astronaut operated the station's robotic arm to move the equipment to the station.

Chapter 6

Down to Earth

After four successful missions and nearly 1,000 hours in space, Ochoa still works for NASA. She is the Deputy Director of Flight Crew Operations. She helps to manage the Astronaut Office and Aircraft Operations.

Ochoa is also married and has two sons. Somehow she still finds time for music, volleyball, and bicycling, her favorite hobbies.

When Ochoa became an astronaut, she also became a role model. She has won many awards. She often speaks to groups about being an astronaut.

Even when she is not in space, Ochoa's job at NASA keeps her busy.

Life Lessons

Ochoa especially enjoys speaking to students. She tells them to study what they enjoy and get a good education. Ochoa learned this lesson from her mother. Education has helped Ochoa achieve many of her goals. She wants to help others achieve theirs too.

In 2002, a middle school in Pasco, Washington, was named for Ochoa. Ochoa met students at the school when it opened. ▼

26

Fast Facts

Full Name: Ellen Ochoa

Birth: May 10, 1958

Hometown: born in Los Angeles, California; moved to
La Mesa, California

Parents: Rosanne and Joseph Ochoa

Siblings: one sister, three brothers

Husband: Coe Fulmer Miles

Children: two sons

Education:
Bachelor of Science in physics, San Diego
State University, 1980
Master of Science in electrical engineering, Stanford
University, 1981
Doctorate in electrical engineering, Stanford
University, 1985

Achievements and Awards:
Outstanding Leadership Medal,
NASA, 1995
Exceptional Service Medal,
NASA, 1997

Time Line

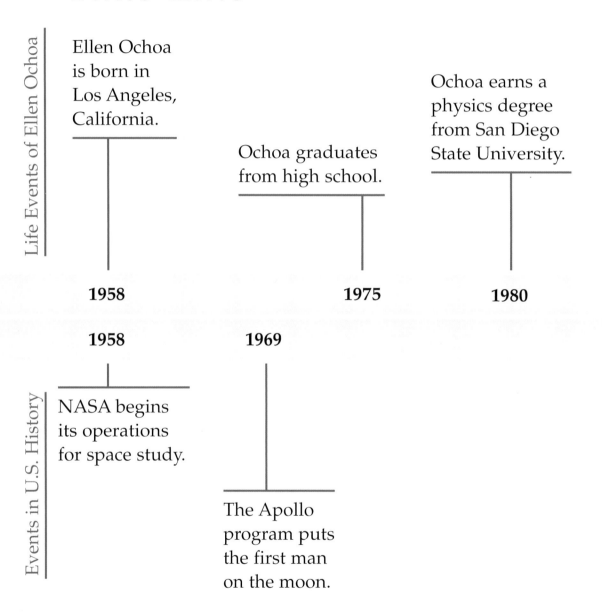

Life Events of Ellen Ochoa

Ellen Ochoa is born in Los Angeles, California.

1958

Ochoa graduates from high school.

1975

Ochoa earns a physics degree from San Diego State University.

1980

Events in U.S. History

1958

NASA begins its operations for space study.

1969

The Apollo program puts the first man on the moon.

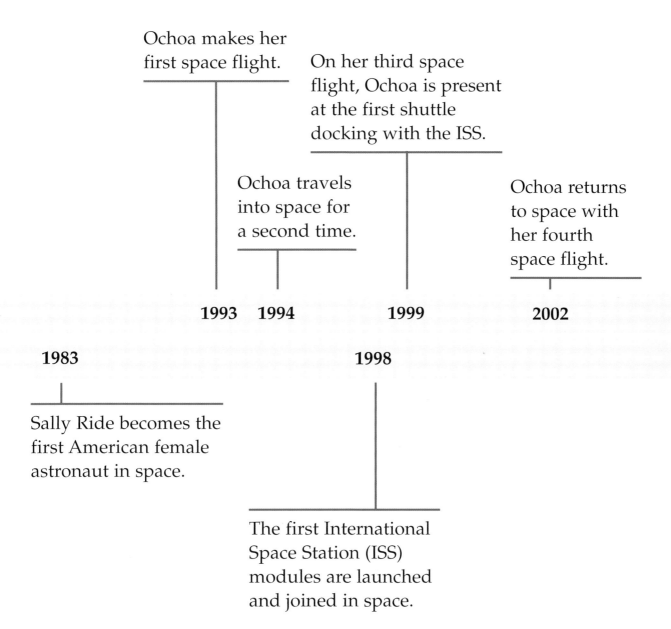

Ochoa makes her first space flight.

On her third space flight, Ochoa is present at the first shuttle docking with the ISS.

Ochoa travels into space for a second time.

Ochoa returns to space with her fourth space flight.

1993   1994   1999   2002

1983   1998

Sally Ride becomes the first American female astronaut in space.

The first International Space Station (ISS) modules are launched and joined in space.

Glossary

International Space Station (in-tur-NASH-uh-nuhl SPAYSS STAY-shuhn)—a scientific laboratory orbiting the earth, built by 16 countries working together

mission specialist (MISH-uhn SPESH-uh-list)—an astronaut trained to carry out experiments and perform space walks

optics (OP-tiks)—an area of physics dealing with the study of light and light waves

patent (PAT-uhnt)—a legal document that protects the rights of inventors to make or sell their inventions

physics (FIZ-iks)—the science that deals with matter and energy; physics includes the study of light, heat, sound, electricity, motion, and force.

satellite (SAT-uh-lite)—a spacecraft that is sent into orbit around the earth, the moon, or another heavenly body

Internet Sites

FactHound offers a safe, fun way to find Internet sites related to this book. All of the sites on FactHound have been researched by our staff.

Here's how:

1. Visit *www.facthound.com*
2. Type in this special code **073685438X** for age-appropriate sites. Or enter a search word related to this book for a more general search.
3. Click on the **Fetch It** button.

FactHound will fetch the best sites for you!

Read More

Iverson, Teresa. *Ellen Ochoa.* Hispanic-American Biographies. Chicago: Raintree, 2005.

Latham, Donna. *Ellen Ochoa: Reach for the Stars.* Defining Moments. New York: Bearport, 2006.

Paige, Joy. *Ellen Ochoa: The First Hispanic Woman in Space.* The Library of Astronaut Biographies. New York: Rosen, 2004.

Index